TEN YEARS : REMEMBERING 9/11

WE WILL NEVER FORGET

TEN YEARS || REMEMBERING 9/11

MARIE TRILLER

JOHN ISAACS BOOKS NEW YORK 2011

CONTENTS

FOREWORD SENATOR KIRSTEN GILLIBRAND

September 11, 2001 was a day that will forever live in the hearts and minds of all Americans, as much for the unbelievable heroism of our first responders and volunteers, as for the devastation of the gravest terrorist attack in our history. In the years following that horrific event, we, as New Yorkers and as Americans, have sought to honor all who died, and the heroic first responders who rushed up the towers to save lives. I was so proud when my colleagues in Congress, Democrats and Republicans, came together to fulfill our undeniable moral obligation, and passed the James Zadroga 9/11 Health and Compensation Act. This legislation ensures proper monitoring and treatment for the men and women who are sick and literally dying from the toxins released at Ground Zero.

In this book, Marie Triller has compiled an inspiring photo-chronicle of 9/11 anniversaries. These photos record nine years of survivors, friends and families, and first responders coming together to memorialize their loved ones. Like our efforts on 9/11 Health, it pays tribute not only to those that lost their lives, but those who continue to honor our heroes' sacrifice.

TEN YEARS : REMEMBERING 9/11

I knew no one who died that day. I couldn't even remember when I had last visited the World Trade Center. But when the towers fell, I was immensely shocked and filled with a sadness I'd never experienced before.

It took two weeks to gather the courage to go to Manhattan and witness the site with my own eyes. Friends would ask me, "How can you go down there?" and I remember thinking, "How can you not?"

I photographed the endless memorials affixed to fences, as well as the crowds, numb with disbelief as the cops shuffled them around the site. I returned a few times. The sorrow was always indescribable.

That Fall, my photographs were included in Here Is New York—A Democracy of Photographs, and The September 11 Photo Project in Soho, New York. Crowds waited on lines for blocks and crammed the spaces to see the photographs by both professionals and amateurs, strung on ceilings and salon-style on walls, free of mats or frames. And when I traveled west the following Summer, and realized that Americans everywhere were mourning 9/11 still, I sent my photographs to universities and asked that the prints be hung as they were in New York, free of art gallery pretension.

Remembering 9/11 became a personal ritual for me; I felt compelled to be witness to every annual ceremony since, where much remains the same. The four aching moments of silence marking the time between the first crash and the fall of the second tower. The sounds of bagpipes, flutes, violins and voices. The tolling bells. Even the sky, more often than not, has the audacity to be stunningly blue and cloudless, as it was that day. And though speeches are given, it is the recitation of names that remains the heart of the memorial.

None of my images was made in the pit at Ground Zero. There were always plenty of press photographers down there, photographing loved ones as they descended the ramps, the images seen in newspapers and magazines. My chosen turf is the periphery, the crowds who gather each September 11 morning, and who tell a truer story of that bright, dark day to me.

—Marie Triller

MEMORY

SECURITY

EXPRESSION

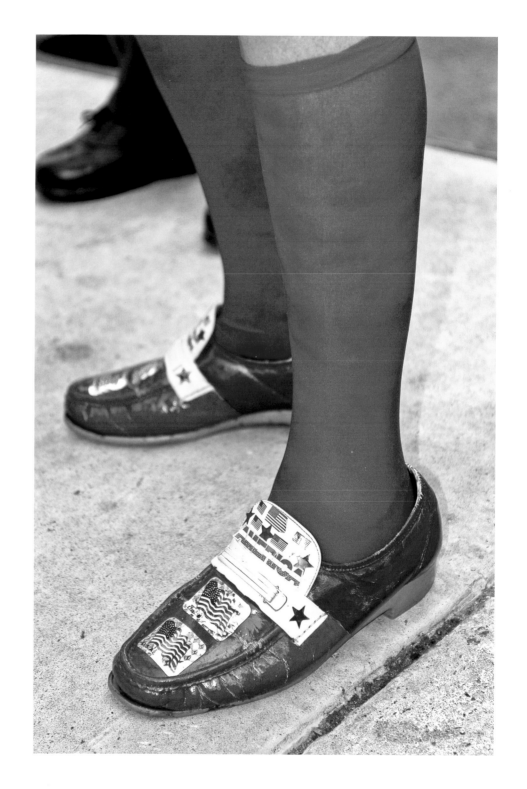

REFLECTION

COMMUNITY

COURAGE

PLACE

JUSTICE

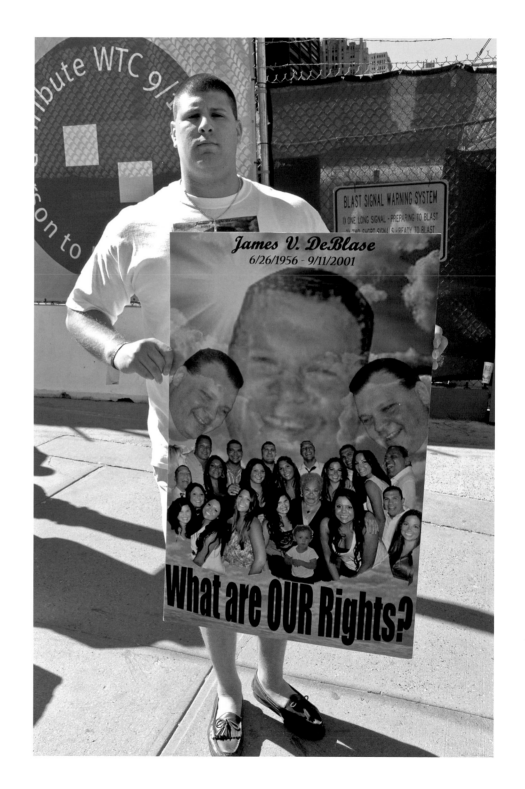

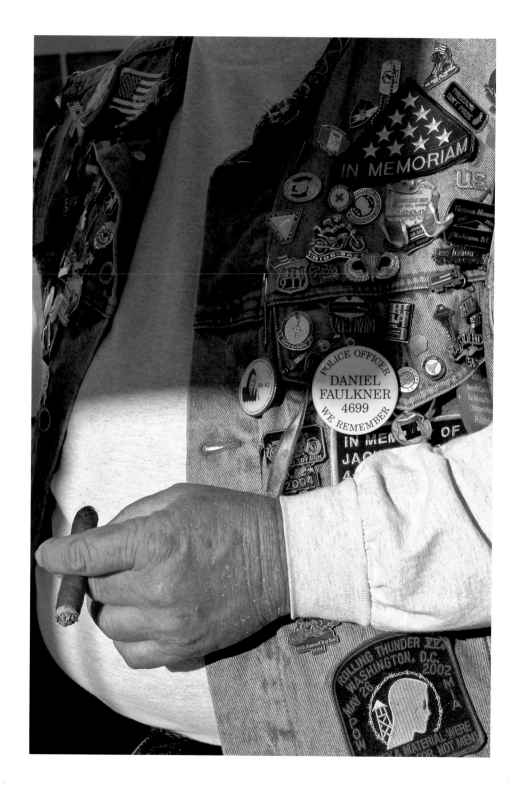

SPIRIT

ICHAEL JOSEPH DUFFY ⚔ THOMAS W. DUFFY ⚔ ANTOINETTE DUGER ⚔ ... CARLOS ... DUGGAN ...
LIS ⚔ VALERIE SILVER ELLIS ⚔ ALBERT ALFY WILLIAM ELMARRY ⚔ EDGAR H. EMERY ⚔ DORIS SUK-YUEN ENG ⚔ CHRISTOPHER
' FARAGHER ⚔ BAT. CHIEF THOMAS FARINO ⚔ NANCY CAROLE FARLEY ⚔ ELIZABETH ANN 'BETTY' FARMER ⚔ DOUGLAS FARR
RAS FERNANDEZ ⚔ ELISA GISELLE FERRAINA ⚔ ANNE MARIE SALLERIN FERREIRA ⚔ ROBERT JOHN FERRIS ⚔ DAVID FRANCIS
LEEN FLECHA ⚔ FIRE MARSHALL ANDRE G. FLETCHER ⚔ CARL FLICKINGER ⚔ FF. JOHN JOSEPH FLORIO ⚔ JOSEPH W. FLOU
REDERICK ⚔ LT. ANDREW A. FREDERICKS ⚔ TAMITHA FREEMEN ⚔ BRETT O. FREIMAN ⚔ LT. PETER L. FREUND ⚔ ARLENE E. FR
, JR. ⚔ CLAUDE MICHAEL GANN ⚔ LT. CHARLES WILLIAM GARBARINI ⚔ CESAR GARCIA ⚔ DAVID GARCIA ⚔ JORGE LUIS MORRO
ENOVESE ⚔ ALAYNE F. GENTUL ⚔ DEP. CHIEF EDWARD F. GERAGHTY ⚔ SUZANNE GERATY ⚔ RALPH GERHARDT ⚔ ROBERT J. GE
MARTIN GIOVINAZZO ⚔ KUM-KUM GIROLAMO ⚔ SALVATORE GITTO ⚔ CYNTHIA GIUGLIANO ⚔ MON GJONBALAJ ⚔ DIANNE GLADSTO
RY GOODY ⚔ KIRAN REDDY GOPU ⚔ CATHERINE CARMEN GORAYEB ⚔ KEREN GORDON ⚔ SEBASTIAN GORKI ⚔ KIERAN GORMAN
FLORENCE M. GREGORY ⚔ DENISE GREGORY ⚔ PEDRO 'DAVID' GREHAN ⚔ JOHN M. GRIFFIN ⚔ TAWANNA GRIFFIN ⚔ JOAN D. G
MARY LOU HAGUE ⚔ LT. DAVID HALDERMAN ⚔ MILE RACHEL HALE ⚔ RICHARD HALL ⚔ VASWALD GEORGE HALL ⚔ ROBERT
RELL ⚔ STEWART D. HARRIS ⚔ AISHA ANNE HARRIS ⚔ JOHN PATRICK HART ⚔ JOHN CLINTON HARTZ ⚔ EMERIC J. HARVEY ⚔ B
CKS ⚔ BRIAN HENNESSEY ⚔ MICHELLE MARIE HENRIQUE ⚔ FF. JOSEPH P. HENRY ⚔ FF. WILLIAM L. HENRY ⚔ JOHN HENWOOD ⚔
OGES ⚔ RONALD GEORGE HOERNER ⚔ PATRICK ALOYSIUS HOEY ⚔ STEPHEN G. HOFFMAN ⚔ MARCIA HOFFMAN ⚔ FREDERICK J. HO
EN HUCZKO ⚔ KRIS R. HUGHES ⚔ MELISSA HARRINGTON HUGHES ⚔ THOMAS F. HUGHES ⚔ TIMOTHY ROBERT HUGHES ⚔ PAUL R. H
⚔ JOHN ISKYAN ⚔ KAZUSHIGE ITO ⚔ ALEKSANDR VALERYERICH IVANTSOV ⚔ VIRGINIA JABLONSKI ⚔ BROOKE ALEXANDRA JA
WILLIAM R. JOHNSTON ⚔ ARTHUR JOSEPH JONES ⚔ ALLISON HORSTMANN JONES ⚔ BRIAN L. JONES ⚔ CHRISTOPHER D. JONE
IRE MARSHALL VINCENT D. KANE ⚔ JOON KOO KANG ⚔ SHELDON R. KANTER ⚔ DEBORAH H. KAPLAN ⚔ ALVIN PETER KAPPEL
L KELLY ⚔ LT. THOMAS RICHARD KELLY ⚔ FF. THOMAS W. KELLY ⚔ TIMOTHY C. KELLY ⚔ WILLIAM HILL KELLY ⚔ ROBERT C. KE
TER A. KLEIN ⚔ ALAN D. KLEINBERG ⚔ KAREN J. KLITZMAN ⚔ PO. RONALD PHILIP KLOEPFER ⚔ YEVGENY KNIAZEV ⚔ THOMAS P
GELA R. KYTE ⚔ AMARNAUTH LACHHMAN ⚔ ANDREW LACORTE ⚔ GANESH LADKAT ⚔ JAMES P. LADLEY ⚔ DANIEL M. VAN LAER
RANDALL LARRABEE ⚔ HAMIDOU S. LARRY ⚔ FF. SCOTT A. LARSEN ⚔ JOHN ADAM LARSON ⚔ GARY E. LASKO ⚔ NICHOLAS C. L
TA LEE ⚔ LORRAINE LEE ⚔ RICHARD Y.C. LEE ⚔ YANG DER LEE ⚔ KATHRYN BLAIR LEE ⚔ STUART 'SOO-JIN' LEE ⚔ LINDA C. LEE
⚔ RALPH M. LICCIARDI ⚔ EDWARD LICHTSCHEIN ⚔ STEVEN B. LILLIANTHAL ⚔ EMT CARLOS R. LILLO ⚔ CRAIG DAMIAN LILORE
STRANGIO ⚔ CHET LOUIE ⚔ STUART SEID LOUIS ⚔ JOSEPH LOVERO ⚔ MICHAEL W. LOWE ⚔ GARRY LOZIER ⚔ JOHN PETER LOZO
LYONS ⚔ MONICA LYONS ⚔ ROBERT FRANCIS MACE ⚔ JAN MACIEJEWSKI ⚔ CATHERINE FAIRFAX MACRAE ⚔ RICHARD B. MADD
MANGANO ⚔ SARA ELIZABETH MANLEY ⚔ DEBRA M. MANNETTA ⚔ TERENCE J. MANNING ⚔ MARION VICTORIA 'VICKIE' MANNIN
CALI ⚔ BERNARD MASCARENHAS ⚔ STEPHEN F. MASIH ⚔ NICHOLAS G. MASSA ⚔ PATRICIA A. CIMAROLI MASSARI ⚔ MICHAEL MA
CARTHUR ⚔ FF. JOHN K. MCAVOY ⚔ KENNETH M. MCBRAYER ⚔ BRENDAN MCCABE ⚔ MICHAEL J. MCCABE ⚔ FF. THOMAS J. N
RTIN MCGOVERN ⚔ BAT. CHIEF WILLIAM J. MCGOVERN ⚔ STACEY S. MCGOWAN ⚔ FRANCIS NOEL MCGUINN ⚔ PATRICK J. MCGU
MCPADDEN ⚔ FF. TERENCE A. MCSHANE ⚔ FF. TIMOTHY PATRICK MCSWEENEY ⚔ FF. MARTIN E. MCWILLIAMS ⚔ ROCCO A. MED
METZ ⚔ JILL A. METZLER ⚔ DAVID ROBERT MEYER ⚔ NURUL HUQ MIAH ⚔ WILLIAM EDWARD MICCIULLI ⚔ MARTIN PAUL MICHELSTE
Z ⚔ LT. PAUL THOMAS MITCHELL ⚔ RICHARD MIUCCIO ⚔ FRANK V. MOCCIA ⚔ BAT. CHIEF LOUIS JOSEPH MODAFFERI ⚔ BOYIE MO
AN ⚔ LINDSAY S. MOREHOUSE ⚔ GEORGE MORELL ⚔ STEVEN P. MORELLO ⚔ FF. VINCENT S. MORELLO ⚔ ARTURO ALVA MORENO
HAEL MULLIGAN ⚔ PETER JAMES MULLIGAN ⚔ MICHAEL JOSEPH MULLIN ⚔ JAMES DONALD MUNHALL ⚔ NANCY MUNIZ ⚔ CARLOS
R ⚔ FRANK JOSEPH NAPLES ⚔ LT. JOHN P. NAPOLITANO ⚔ CATHERINE A. NARDELLA ⚔ MARIO NARDONE ⚔ MANIKA NARULA ⚔ NA
TROY EDWARD NILSEN ⚔ PAUL R. NIMBLEY ⚔ JOHN BALLANTINE NIVEN ⚔ KATHERINE 'KATIE' MCGARRY NOACK ⚔ CURTIS TERRE
MES ANDREW O'GRADY ⚔ FF. JOSEPH JAY OGREN ⚔ LT. THOMAS G. O'HAGAN ⚔ FF. SAMUEL P. OITICE ⚔ FF. PATRICK O'KEEFE

AFTERWORD ELEANOR HEARTNEY

September 11, 2011 is one of those watershed days, altering the lives, not only of the victims' families, but of all who lived through it. For many of us, it was the real beginning of the 21st century, ushering in a new world where social, political and personal connections were dramatically altered in ways that are still unfolding. But for all the clarity of our memories of that day, it is still far from apparent what it meant and continues to mean. How does one commemorate an event like 9/11? How does one disentangle the threads of grief, alarm, empathy, heroism, solace, helplessness and rage? How does one move on from the myriad emotions of that day in ways that point toward a more hopeful future?

Marie Triller's *Ten Years: Remembering 9/11* offers insight into these questions. Begun spontaneously as a photographer's personal response to a catastrophe that unfolded in her home state, it grew into a multiyear project documenting the crowds flocking to Ground Zero on each of the succeeding anniversaries. Conceived without any political agenda, this series of photographs became one person's way to make sense of unspeakable tragedy. But the images also transcend their creator. The extremely diverse set of individuals who come to mourn and to remember are a microcosm of a larger psychic community uniting us all across national and international borders on that most affecting of anniversaries.

It has now been ten years since the destruction of the World Trade Towers. While time has blunted some of the sharpest sensations evoked by that event, it has not produced a homogeneous response. Instead, as Triller discovered when she took her camera down to Ground Zero each year, the range of participants' emotions were as varied in year two as in year ten. As a result, the photographs here are not presented in a chronological fashion, but according to a set of themes that reveal the contradictory feelings of patriotism, anger, resignation, hope, forgiveness and fear that pull at those who pause to remember.

Thus, for instance, the photographs grouped within the category of MEMORY offer the somber faces of those who reflect on the individual lives lost in the tragedy ten years ago. EXPRESSION presents the outpouring of creative energy harnessed by individuals attempting to make sense of this nearly incomprehensible event. JUSTICE suggests the many ways that people have tried to understand the moral meaning of this tragedy. SPIRIT reflects the way that people reach out to higher powers in the face of otherwise incomprehensible tragedy.

Sometimes the expressions on people's faces are heartbreaking. In other images where mourners cover their faces or bow their heads the expression we don't see is even more affecting. For some of those gathered at Ground Zero, these anniversaries provide opportunities to make political statements —one sign held aloft calls for revenge against Osama bin Laden, while others plead for non-violence and peace. A number of conspiracy theories are aired, as are religious calls for repentance. The dead are evoked in photographs, with the presentations of their names and through impromptu shrines. Flags and flag motifs abound – they appear as rippling reflections in the windows of buildings surrounding Ground Zero, are painted on vehicles, made into lapel ribbons and incorporated into floral wreaths, clothing and murals. There are lighter moments, as when a group of school children in flag t-shirts beam broadly for the camera. Taken together, this series shows how the 9/11 anniversaries are experienced individually and collectively, in anguish and reconciliation.

Ten Years: Remembering 9/11 reveals that 9/11 was not a single event. Because it is inscribed in multiple memories, it lives on in our imaginations in innumerable ways. Dispassionately presenting the faces and reactions of people touched by this event, Triller suggests that time and remembrance are like a river. They flow through our lives, ebbing and surging, but never completely retreating. In keeping with this realization, her moving photographs document the process by which this terrible day has been rewoven into the fabric of our lives.

Publication © 2011 Marie Triller
Foreword © 2011 Senator Kirsten Gillibrand
Afterword © 2011 Eleanor Heartney
Images © 2011 Marie Triller

Published on the occasion of the Tenth Anniversary of the 9/11 Attacks on the United States.

Book design by John Isaacs

Printed and bound by Capital Offset Company, Concord NH

Published by John Isaacs Books
Willowdale Farm Claverack NY 12513 USA

ISBN 978-0-9772971-8-4